WOW IN THE WORLD

TWO WHATS?! AND A WOW!

THINK & TINKER ~~WORKBOOK~~ PLAY

Activities and Games for Curious Kids

BY MINDY THOMAS AND GUY RAZ

Houghton Mifflin Harcourt
Boston New York

The authors would like to thank Thomas van Kalken, Anna Zagorski, Rebecca Caban, Jessica Boddy, Anthony Knight, Jack Teagle, Meredith Halpern-Ranzer, Mary Claire Cruz, Marissa Asuncion, Amy Cloud, and Steven Malk.

hmhbooks.com

The text was set in Benton Sans.
Cover design by Mary Claire Cruz
Interior design by Marissa Asuncion

Library of Congress Cataloging in Publication Data is available.
ISBN: 978-0-358-47015-1

Manufactured in United States of America
DOC 10 9 8 7 6 5 4 3 2 1
4500799950

Welcome to Two Whats and a Wow, a game show you can play IN A BOOK!
That's right — A PLAYBOOK!

In this playbook, you'll find 37 rounds of Two Whats?! And a Wow! In each round, we list three odd, interesting, and unusual statements on a scientific theme. Only one of these statements is a *true* WOW. The other two? Just a couple of made up WHAAAAATS?! It's up to YOU to flex your mind muscles to identify the one *true* WOW. Once you've made your guess, just flip the page, and the correct answer will be revealed! (Don't forget to give yourself a drumroll before the big reveal!)

But that's not all . . .

After each round, we leave you with a little scientific challenge to keep the Wow rolling. Most of these challenges require odds and ends you already have at home, and *all* of these challenges are best shared with a friend or family member. *It's important to have someone there to catch your eyeballs when they pop out of your head from all that Wowing!*

We hope you have as much fun playing with this book as we had making it. Now go forth and find those Wows!

Mindy & Guy

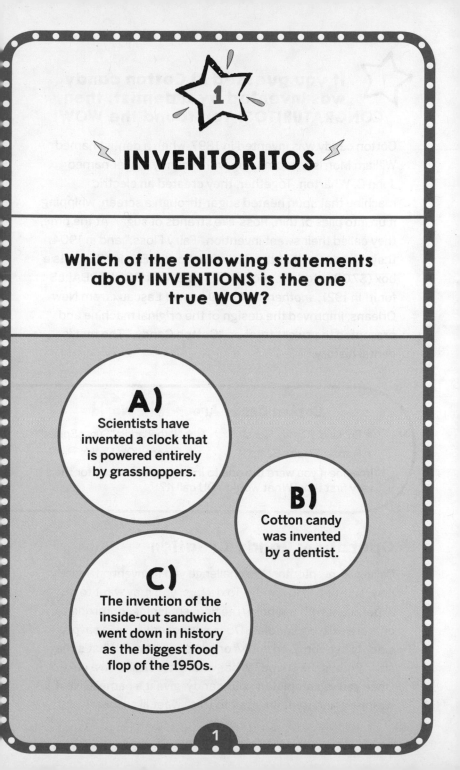

⚡ INVENTORITOS ⚡

1

Which of the following statements about INVENTIONS is the one true WOW?

A)
Scientists have invented a clock that is powered entirely by grasshoppers.

B)
Cotton candy was invented by a dentist.

C)
The invention of the inside-out sandwich went down in history as the biggest food flop of the 1950s.

1

1 If you guessed B) Cotton candy was invented by a dentist, then CONGRATURITOS! You found the WOW!

Cotton candy was invented in 1897, when a dentist named William Morrison teamed up with a candy maker named John C. Wharton. Together, they created an electric machine that spun heated sugar through a screen, whipping it up into piles of thin, floss-like strands of sugar. At the time, they called their sweet invention "Fairy Floss," and in 1904, they introduced it at the St. Louis World's Fair for 25 cents a box ($7.00 in today's money). People went BONKERBALLS for it! In 1921, *another* dentist, Dr. Josef Lascaux from New Orleans, improved the design of the original machine and presented the sweet treat as "Cotton Candy." The rest is dental history.

Cotton Candy Around the World

★ England: "Candy Floss"
★ France: "Papa's Beard"
★ Netherlands: "Sugar Spider"
★ Greece: "Old Ladies' Hair"

Imagine if you were the one to invent cotton candy for the very first time. What would YOU call it?

Operation: Candy Creation

Calling all inventoritos! We challenge you to invent an entirely new, one-of-a kind candy! To do this, you may want to experiment with melting, freezing, smashing, or mixing two or more existing candies. Does your candy have a savory side? Is it gummy, crumbly, or not-so-yummy? What's the size? What's the shape? What would it look like on a cake? Once you've completed your candy, give it a name! Give it a wrapper! And treat yourself to this sweet lil snacker!

GIRAFFE GAFFES AND FACTS

Which of the following statements about GIRAFFES is the one true WOW?

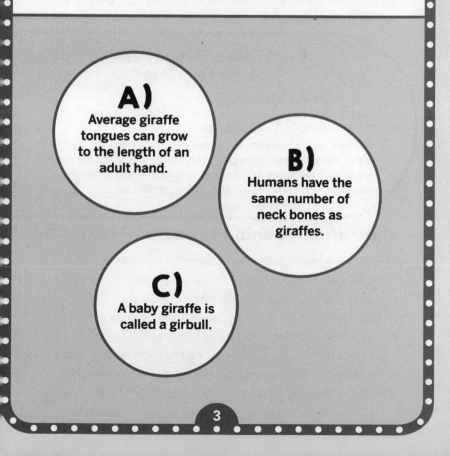

A) Average giraffe tongues can grow to the length of an adult hand.

B) Humans have the same number of neck bones as giraffes.

C) A baby giraffe is called a girbull.

If you guessed B) Humans have the same number of neck bones as giraffes, then CONGRATURITOS! You found the WOW!

With their strong long necks stretching 15 feet (4.6 m) into the tree canopies of Africa, you wouldn't think that a giraffe neck had anything in common with a human neck, but guess again! It turns out that giraffes have the same number of bones in their necks as humans. Both human and giraffe necks are made up of seven vertebrae. Vertebrae are bones that run from your head to your hips, and they make up what's known as the vertebral column. But while a human neck bone measures around half an inch in length, a single giraffe's vertebrae can grow to be over 10 inches (25 cm) long!

How to Sleep Like a Giraffe in Three Easy Steps

Step 1: Assume a standing position.
Step 2: Snooze with one eye open and both ears alert.
Step 3: Wake up 5 minutes later.

Giraffes are considered to be some of the strangest sleepers in the animal kingdom, sleeping in spurts for a total of anywhere between 30 minutes and 4 hours a night! Do you or someone you know have any interesting sleeping habits?

Operation: Leaning Tower of Neck!

Measuring in at six feet long, adult giraffe necks are about the same length as some adult humans' entire bodies! Try building your own six foot (1.8 m) giraffe neck using stackable things from around your home. A column of canned foods? A tower of blocks? Test which materials work best to help you reach new heights. Once you finish, be sure to give your giraffe neck a head and a name, and introduce your family to your new, long-necked pet.

FREEZING FACTOIDS AND FALLACIES

Which of the following frozen statements about ANTARCTICA is the one true WOW?

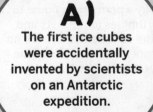

A) The first ice cubes were accidentally invented by scientists on an Antarctic expedition.

B) Ice skating Olympic hopefuls from around the world travel to Antarctica for training every year.

C) Antarctica is actually a desert.

3 If you guessed C) Antarctica is actually a desert, then CONGRATURITOS! You found the WOW!

When you think of a desert, you probably imagine a blistering sun hanging in the sky, boundless sand dunes stretching toward the horizon, and maybe a palm tree. But not all deserts are hot. In fact, the largest desert in the world is found in Antarctica! This is because deserts aren't measured by heat or grains of sand. What makes a desert a desert is how much rain the region receives per year. And in Antarctica, it rains less than 2 inches (51 mm) each year on average. By comparison, New York City receives an average of 51 inches (1,295 mm) of rain a year!

That's it! I'm moving to Antarctica!

Not so fast! Antarctica is actually a permanent home to . . . NO ONE! While there are opportunities for tourists and researchers to spend time on the continent, there are no cities or towns set up for permanent residents. Imagine what it would take for you to move your family to icy Antarctica and set up a home!

Operation: Ice Age

Freeze some small waterproof objects into ice cubes overnight. The next morning, attempt to free these objects by melting the ice cubes using different materials found in the kitchen, such as salt, pepper, cornmeal, and food coloring. Notice the effect each of these items has on the ice cubes. Which ones melt the easiest?

EAR, THERE, AND EVERYWHERE

Which of the following statements about EARS is the one true WOW?

A) In the 16th century, earwax was used to fill cavities.

B) Grasshoppers have ears on their bellies.

C) Humans have better hearing than pigeons.

If you guessed B) Grasshoppers have ears on their bellies, then CONGRATURITOS! You found the WOW!

Imagine having to stick an earphone in your bellybutton just to listen to your favorite song. Well, if you were a grasshopper, that might not be too far from the truth! As strange as it may sound, grasshoppers actually have ears on their abdomens, tucked away under their wings. Scientists believe this allows grasshoppers to better hear the chirps of their fellow grasshoppers.

Do Your Ears Hang Low?

Monte Pierce holds the Guinness World Record for the World's Longest Earlobes Stretched. Just how long are these lobes? Monte is able to stretch his earlobes to a length of 5 inches (13 cm) for his left and 4.5 inches (11 cm) for his right. It should come as no surprise that these lengthy lobes also hold the record for greatest ear slingshot!

Operation: Can You Hear Me Now?

Our five senses—sight, taste, touch, hearing, and smell—help us to interpret the world we live in. But what if we lost one of these senses and had to rely more heavily on another? While wearing a blindfold over your eyes, have a partner test your sense of hearing by asking you to identify certain mystery sounds: jingling keys, a zipper on a coat, a loud piece of velcro, or other sounds that are tough to decipher on their own! When you're finished, swap roles and play another round!

OUT OF THIS WORLD

Which of the following statements about the SOLAR SYSTEM is the one true WOW?

A) Earth can fit inside Jupiter's Great Red Spot.

B) Some scientists believe our moon was "burped" into Earth's orbit by a black hole.

C) Uranus is bubbling with gas volcanoes.

5. If you guessed A) Earth can fit inside Jupiter's Great Red Spot, then CONGRATURITOS! You found the WOW!

Jupiter is the largest planet in our solar system by A LOT! In fact, Jupiter is 11 times wider than Earth! One of Jupiter's most striking features, its Great Red Spot, is large enough to fit an entire Earth inside of it. But—and this is a big but!—because Jupiter is made out of gas rather than a solid material like Earth, this Great Red Spot is constantly changing in size and shape. Just over a century ago, you could fit THREE Earths inside of it.

Take Only Pictures, Leave Only Footprints

On July 20, 1969, Apollo 11 Astronaut Neil Armstrong left the first footprint on the moon. And because there is no wind or rain on the moon, if you were to visit it today—or even a million years from now—you would find that same footprint exactly where Neil left it, perfectly preserved. You may or may not get a chance to leave your own footprint on the moon, but you *do* have a chance to leave your mark right here on Earth! How will *you* make a positive impact that could last for millions of years to come?

Operation: Spot the Space Station!

The International Space Station orbits around planet Earth every 90 minutes. That's 16 times a day that it whizzes around at a whopping speed of 5 miles-per-*second* (8 km-per-second)! And since it's the third brightest object in the sky, it's easy to spot with the naked eye. We challenge you and your grownup to visit www.spotthestation.nasa.gov together, and find out exactly when the International Space Station will be whizzing over YOU!

⚡ CRUSTACEAN STATION ⚡

Which of the following statements about CRUSTACEANS is the one true WOW?

A)
Hermit crabs will find "roommates" if their shells are too large.

B)
Shrimp are born with tiny feet that fall off during the first few days of their lives.

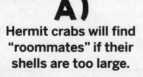

C)
Lobsters have teeth in their stomach and pee out of their eyes.

6

If you guessed C) Lobsters have teeth in their stomach and pee out of their eyes, then CONGRATURITOS! You found the WOW!

Believe it or not, it's all true! Lobsters actually have TWO stomachs. The first stomach, located just behind the lobster's eyes, contains little teeth that grind up the food before passing it off to the second stomach for digestion. Lobsters also have small openings, called urine-release nozzles, located right under their eyeballs, and sometimes they will even pee in each other's faces as a way of communicating! Would you rather chew with your stomach OR pee out of your face?

Golfster Ball?

Researchers from the University of Maine found a way to take discarded lobster shells and turn them into biodegradable golf balls. The bad news is that these balls only go about 70 percent of the distance of a regular golf ball. The good news is that these golf balls are ideal for golfing on cruise ships!

Operation: Shell-o!

The hermit crab is a little unusual for a crustacean in that its behind is covered in a soft exoskeleton. And since this exoskeleton doesn't offer the protection it needs, the hermit crab must find a protective shell in which to live! We challenge you to find a cardboard box and transform it into your own personal hermit crab shell! Like a hermit crab, you'll need to squeeze into your "shell" backwards, holding the box to your body with your back feet, while using your front feet (arms) to help pull you around! Live that hermit crab lifestyle (for a day . . . or 5 minutes)!

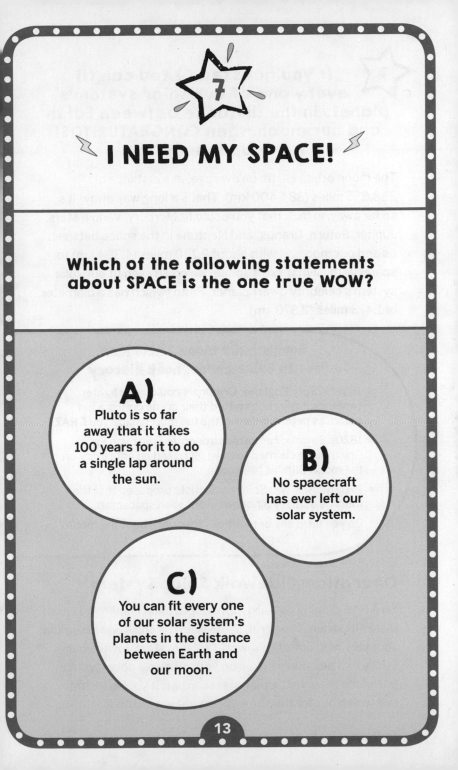

7

⚡ I NEED MY SPACE! ⚡

Which of the following statements about SPACE is the one true WOW?

A)
Pluto is so far away that it takes 100 years for it to do a single lap around the sun.

B)
No spacecraft has ever left our solar system.

C)
You can fit every one of our solar system's planets in the distance between Earth and our moon.

7 If you guessed C) You can fit every one of our solar system's planets in the distance between Earth and our moon, then CONGRATURITOS! You found the WOW!

The moon orbits Earth, on average, at a distance of 238,855 miles (384,400 km). That's a long way away! It's so far away, in fact, that you could fit Mercury, Venus, Mars, Jupiter, Saturn, Uranus, and Neptune in the space between us and our moon . . . with about 2,730 miles (4,394 km) to spare! With all that extra space, we could even fit our solar system's celebrity dwarf planet, Pluto (which has a diameter of 1,473 miles (2,370 km).

Bonkerballs Moon Theories Proven False throughout History

★ 18th-century England: Criminals could get a lighter sentence if they committed their crime during a full moon, as people believed the full moon made you CRAZY!

★ 1820s Bavaria: Famous astronomer Franz von Paula Gruithuisen claimed to have glimpsed an entire city on the moon with his telescope.

★ 1970 Russia: Two Soviet scientists proposed that the moon is actually a hollowed-out alien spacecraft.

Do you have any bonkerballs theories about the moon?

Operation: Sidewalk Solar System

Do a little digging to learn more about each planet and what makes it unique. Then grab some sidewalk chalk and assemble your very own out-of-this-world solar system. Invite your family to a planetary picnic on your sidewalk solar system. Introduce them to the planets, share what you've learned, and watch out for the sun—you might get burned!

8

⚡ SINKING STRUCTURES ⚡

Which of the following statements about STRUCTURES is the one true WOW?

A)
Venice, a city in Italy, is sinking at a rate of 1 inch (2.5 cm) per year.

B)
The Eiffel Tower in Paris, France, shrinks 6 inches (15 cm) each winter.

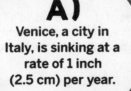

C)
The Empire State building in New York City had two floors removed in 1938.

8 If you guessed B) The Eiffel Tower in Paris, France, shrinks 6 inches (15 cm) each winter, then CONGRATURITOS! You found the WOW!

The Eiffel Tower stands in the heart of Paris at a staggering 1,063 feet (324 m) tall. However, in cooler months the tower shrinks as much as 6 inches (15 cm). This is because of a phenomenon known as thermal expansion, which happens when certain materials, like steel, expand in the heat and contract in the cold. During the summer, temperatures in Paris can reach as high as 105 degrees Fahrenheit (41 degrees Celsius)! This extreme heat causes the base of the tower to expand and boosts its overall height. When the winter months roll in, the tower contracts, or shrinks back down to its original height.

Built to Last

The Eiffel Tower was built as part of the 1889 World's Fair, a big festival celebrating the achievements of different countries. Here's what else has been built for the World's Fair over the years:

★ 1939: Golden Gate Bridge and Bay Bridge, San Francisco

★ 1962: The Space Needle, Seattle

★ 1986: Canada Place, Vancouver

What giant structure would *you* build to celebrate the World's Fair?

Operation: Make a Mini Model!

Construct your own mini model of a famous structure such as the Golden Gate Bridge, Taj Mahal, or Eiffel Tower! Toothpicks, Popsicle sticks, or cotton swabs all make for great miniature building materials.

ANIMAL AVENGERS

Which of the following statements about ANIMAL SUPERPOWERS is the one true WOW?

A) The mantis shrimp can throw a left hook faster than a speeding bullet.

B) The viper snake can smell its prey from over 12 feet (3.7 m) away using the tip of its tail.

C) Dung beetles can lift more than 2,000 times their own body weight.

If you guessed A) The mantis shrimp can throw a left hook faster than a speeding bullet, then CONGRATURITOS! You found the WOW!

The proud owner of the fastest fists on the planet is the mantis shrimp, swinging its club-like fists at speeds of over 50 miles per hour (23 m per second). But this vicious left hook isn't the result of powerful muscles. Instead, the mantis shrimp's arm is naturally spring-loaded, meaning all it has to do is sit back, wait for an unsuspecting crustacean to swim by, cock its arm back, and BAM! It's lights out!

Who You Callin' a Shrimp?!

The mantis shrimp can also:

★ Create flashes of heat that are hotter than the surface of the sun.

★ Use its claws as barbed spears when hunting.

★ Judge distances precisely with just one eye.

Which of the mantis shrimp's superpowers would you want?

Operation: Pack-a-Punch!

We challenge you to construct a Popsicle-stick catapult!

What you'll need: nine wide Popsicle sticks, three rubber bands, a bottle top, and some glue (or strong tape)

Wow-to:

1. Place seven Popsicle sticks in a stack. Twist a rubber band around each end.

2. Place one Popsicle stick across the top of the stack and one right below the stack, making a cross shape.

3. Twist the second rubber band around the middle of the cross. Place the final rubber band around the bottom of these two sticks.

4. Attach the bottle top to the non-banded end using glue or tape.

5. Experiment launching tiny objects off of your new catapult!

10

⚡ PESKY PESTS ⚡

Which of the following statements about PESKY ANIMALS is the one true WOW?

A)
Squirrels are one of the leading causes of power outages in the United States.

B)
Over 5,000 moose are involved in traffic accidents in Sweden each year.

C)
More rats live in New York City than people.

If you guessed A) Squirrels are one of the leading causes of power outages in the United States, then CONGRATURITOS! You found the WOW!

One of the greatest threats to the United States' power grid has a big bushy tail and two buck teeth. Although it's tricky to track exactly how many power outages are caused by these furry little rodents every year, one estimate puts the figure at a whopping 3,500, with 400 squirrel-related outages reported in Austin, Texas, alone! Although damage caused by squirrel attacks can be fixed a lot more quickly than that caused by extreme weather events, it's still costly. In 2015, squirrel attacks cost the state of Montana more than $11 million! How NUTS is that?!

Pesky Pests

Squirrels are considered a pest in the United States. But other countries have their own pesky pests:

★ England: Badgers
★ Australia: Camels
★ Kenya: Elephants
★ India: Monkeys

What animals do you see causing a nuisance and being a PEST?

Operation: Bird Feeder or Nut Hut!?

If there's one thing squirrels seem to love more than chewing on power lines, it's invading bird feeders! We challenge you to put your engineering skills to the test by creating a squirrel-proof bird feeder. Collect materials from around your home or recycling bin to create your feeder. As you design, consider the perspectives of both squirrels and birds. Prepare for lots of trial and error, and don't forget the birdseed!

11

⚡ AROUND THE HOUSE ⚡

Which of the following statements about HOUSEHOLD ITEMS is the one true WOW?

A)
The microwave oven was invented for military purposes.

B)
The toaster is named after one of its three inventors.

C)
Bubble wrap was originally designed to be used as wallpaper.

11 ⭐ If you guessed C) Bubble wrap was originally designed to be used as wallpaper, then CONGRATURITOS! You found the WOW!

You might know it as that packaging material that goes POP POP POP, but the inventors of bubble wrap, Alfred Fielding and Marc Chavannes, had a very different plan for their creation: WALLPAPER! It wasn't until 4 years after their original idea that they approached the computer manufacturer IBM and pitched the idea of using their invention to pack and protect computers for shipping. IBM agreed and started using bubble wrap to safeguard their fragile equipment as they packed it up and shipped it off. The rest is plastic poppin' history!

Happy Accidents

Bubble wrap wasn't the only thing that was invented by accident!

★ Play-Doh was originally sold as a wallpaper cleaner.

★ Post-it notes were invented partly by accident as the result of a glue that was considered too weak to be useful.

★ Slinkys were invented when a naval engineer accidentally dropped some coiled wires off his worktable, only to see them flop end-to-end across the floor rather than spring back up.

What discoveries have YOU stumbled across by accident?

Operation: Double Duty

Come up with an uncommon use for a common household object. Experiment with things like old swimming pool noodles, salad tongs, or those little tabs that keep bags of bread closed. Imagine seeing these items for the first time. How would you put them to use?

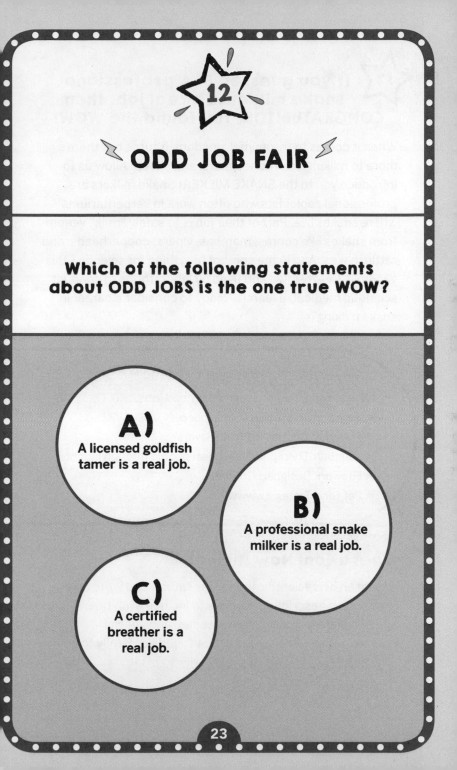

12

⚡ ODD JOB FAIR ⚡

Which of the following statements about ODD JOBS is the one true WOW?

A)
A licensed goldfish tamer is a real job.

B)
A professional snake milker is a real job.

C)
A certified breather is a real job.

12 If you guessed B) A professional snake milker is a real job, then CONGRATURITOS! You found the WOW!

When it comes to the animal kingdom, it turns out there's more to milking than cows, goats, and sheep. Allow us to introduce you to the SNAKE MILKER! Snake milkers are professional zoologists who often work in serpentariums where snakes live. Part of their job is to safely "milk" venom from snakes like cobras, mambas, vipers, copperheads, and rattlesnakes! And in the spirit of "anything for science," this venom is freeze-dried and used by laboratories to conduct scientific medical research. Ready to consider a career in snake milking?

Anything for Science!

Here are some other scientifically odd jobs:

★ Scatologist: Studies animal poop
★ Flavorist: Creates artificial flavors
★ Laughter Therapist: Helps heal people through laughter
★ Firework Designer: Ooooh!
★ Pet Food Taster: Ewwww!

Operation: Now Hiring!

Create an odd scientific job for the future, and write up a creative job description. Be sure to include a job title, specific duties, qualifications needed, and special responsibilities. See if you can get friends or family to apply!

13

⚡ INTERGALACTIC ⚡ ROAD TRIP

Which of the following statements about SPACE TRAVEL is the one true WOW?

A)
It would take roughly only 1 hour for you to drive to space in your car.

B)
The space shuttle Discovery had six cupholders in the cockpit alone.

C)
It would take 53 years to travel to Mars in a 747 airplane.

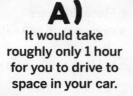

If you guessed A) It would take roughly only I hour for you to drive to space in your car, then CONGRATURITOS! You found the WOW!

That's right—if your family car wasn't held back by pesky things like gravity and dynamic thrust, then you, too, could take a trip out of our atmosphere and into outer space, and it would take you only around an hour to get there! The Kármán Line, the border that separates Earth's atmosphere from outer space, is located about 62 miles (100 km) above sea level. Meaning that if your magical space-ready car were driving at a steady pace of 60 mph (97 kmph), it would take you around an hour to get there.

Are We There Yet?

Here's how long it would take to get to Mars depending on mode of transport:

★ Walking: 4,000 years
★ Car: 228 years, driving 70 mph (113 kmph)
★ Plane: 32 years
★ Rocket ship: 243 days

Imagine being onboard a rocket to Mars. How would YOU pass the time?

Operation: 3 . . . 2 . . . I . . . BLASTOFF!

Challenge a few friends or family members to a blast-off balloon race! First, find a wide open space and different colored balloons for each challenger. Next, have each person inflate their balloon by blowing air from their lungs until it's at maximum capacity. Then, pinch the end of the balloon to keep the air from seeping out. Finally, hold your balloons over your heads and commence in a group countdown, "3 . . . 2 . . . I . . . BLASTOFF!" Launch your balloons into the atmosphere, and then measure where they land to see whose balloon made the most distance.

⚡ MONEY, MONEY, MONEY ⚡

Which of the following statements about MONEY is the one true WOW?

A)
For close to 100 years, Vikings used fish heads as money when traveling.

B)
British coins were originally crafted out of old buttons.

C)
Chocolate was used as currency in some ancient South American civilizations.

If you guessed C) Chocolate was used as currency in some ancient South American civilizations, then CONGRATURITOS! You found the WOW!

Today, a block of chocolate might make for a tasty treat, but to certain ancient cultures like the Aztecs or the Mayans, it was worth so much more! Like a lot of early civilizations, the Mayan and Aztec people of Central and South America didn't use coins as money. Instead, they traded items like tobacco, maize, and clothing for everything they needed. However, among all the things that were traded, few items were as prized as the roasted cacao bean: the basis of everything chocolate. In fact, early Spanish colonial accounts from the 16th century show that Europeans used roasted cacao beans to pay indigenous tribes from both civilizations!

Currencies of the World

★ United Kingdom: Pound sterling

★ Vietnam: Dong

★ Poland: Zloty

★ South Korea: Won

Imagine creating your own currency. What would YOU call it?

Operation: Clean Money

What you'll need: pennies, small bowls or cups, and acidic substances like vinegar, lemon juice, orange juice, ketchup, or soda

Wow-to:

1. Fill each bowl or cup with a different substance.
2. Place a penny in each bowl or cup and leave them overnight.
3. Observe which acidic substances, if any, leave your penny looking as good as new!

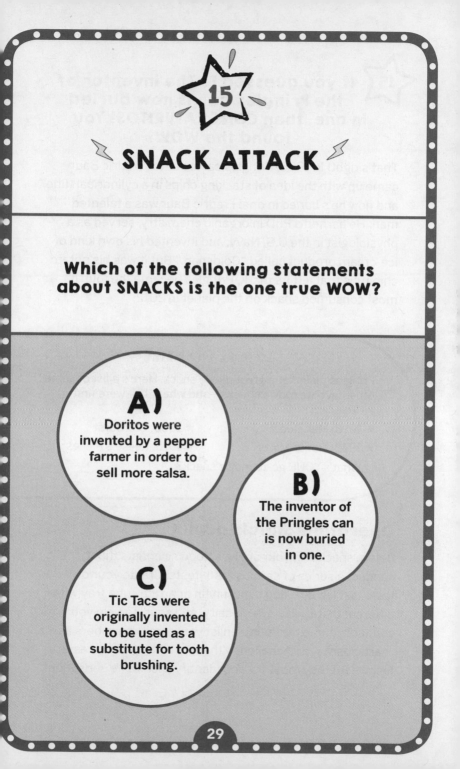

15

⚡ SNACK ATTACK ⚡

Which of the following statements about SNACKS is the one true WOW?

A)
Doritos were invented by a pepper farmer in order to sell more salsa.

B)
The inventor of the Pringles can is now buried in one.

C)
Tic Tacs were originally invented to be used as a substitute for tooth brushing.

If you guessed B) The inventor of the Pringles can is now buried in one, then CONGRATURITOS! You found the WOW!

That's right! In 1966, Pringles can inventor Fredric Baur came up with the idea of stacking chips in a cylindrical tube, and now he's *buried* in one! Fredric Baur was a talented man. He earned a PhD in organic chemistry, served as a physiologist in the U.S. Navy, and invented his own kind of ice-cream product called "Coldsnap." But it was his potato chip tube that left its mark. Pringles became the fourth most consumed snack on the planet in 2012.

Love at First Bite

Pringles make for a great movie snack. Here's a list of some other favorite movie snacks—and when they were first introduced!

★ 1926: Milk Duds   ★ 1960: Starburst

★ 1949: Junior Mints   ★ 1978: Reese's Pieces

What's YOUR go-to movie snack?

Operation: Snacktacular

Before snacks hit your shelves, food scientists must conduct a series of serious taste tests. Create your own taste test lab by filling a muffin tin or an ice cube tray with different tastes, like sweet, salty, and sour. To help you conduct your experiment, enlist your family members as "participants" and challenge them to a blindfolded taste test where they must try and identify each taste sensation!

COLORFUL WOWS

Which of the following statements about COLOR is the one true WOW?

A)
The human eye is able to distinguish green more than any other color.

B)
Mosquitoes are attracted to lighter colors.

C)
Blue is the first color human babies are able to recognize.

16 If you guessed A) The human eye is able to distinguish green more than any other color, then CONGRATURITOS! You found the WOW!

Shamrock, seafoam, olive, lime—there are many different shades of green. As it turns out, the human eye can detect more shades of green than any other color. Scientists think one reason why we can perceive or recognize so many different shades of green is because it helped our ancestors decide which plants were safest to eat.

Red and Yellow Making You Hungry?

When it comes to the psychology of color, studies suggest that red makes you hungry and yellow makes you happy. See how many restaurants you can find that use this "ketchup and mustard" combo in their branding, advertising, and restaurant decor. Be sure to take notes on whether this combo has any effect on your appetite!

Operation: Color Mixing Lab

What you'll need: Red, yellow, and blue food coloring; water; an ice cube tray; and clear bowls or containers

Wow-to:

1. Mix the food coloring and water in an ice cube tray and put it in the freezer to make red, yellow, and blue ice cubes.

2. Set up your mixing lab with several clear bowls or containers filled with water.

3. Experiment! Mix different combinations of these red, yellow, and blue ice cubes in each bowl or container, and notice the new colors that emerge!

HAIR WE GO!

Which of the following statements about HAIR is the one true WOW?

A)
On average, humans lose 300 strands of hair in a day.

B)
Wearing a hat can prevent your hair from growing.

C)
The only parts of your skin that don't grow hair are your lips, palms, and soles of your feet.

17 If you guessed C) The only parts of your skin that don't grow hair are your lips, palms, and soles of your feet, then CONGRATURITOS! You found the WOW!

Hair, hair, it's everywhere, whether you can see it there, or not. Well, ALMOST everywhere. There are three places on your human body where hair cannot and will not grow: your lips, your palms, and the soles of your feet. This is due to the fact that these parts are covered in a follicle-free type of skin called glabrous skin. It's smoother than hairy skin and provides padding for the places on your body that need it the most!

Hair Today, Gone Tomorrow

During the Victorian era, fashionistas would create "mourning jewelry" out of locks of hair from their lost loved ones (dead people and pets). This was considered a loving way to remember and honor those who had passed. Have you ever saved a lock of hair for sentimental reasons?

Operation: Hair Detective

On average, humans lose anywhere from 50–100 strands of hair per day. Using a microscope or a magnifying glass, examine a strand of fallen-out hair up close. See if you can get any family members to offer up one of their locks too. Notice the differences (and similarities) between the textures and colors. Hair . . . We . . . Gooooooo!

18

⚡ SAVE IT FOR A ⚡ RAINY DAY

Which of the following statements about weather is the one true WOW?

A)
Tornadoes never occur in lakes, rivers, or oceans.

B)
It takes roughly 2 minutes for a raindrop to hit the ground after forming.

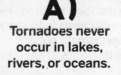

C)
Lightning never strikes in the same place twice.

18 ⭐ If you guessed B) It takes roughly 2 minutes for a raindrop to hit the ground after forming, then CONGRATURITOS! You found the WOW!

Next time you feel those first few drops of rain land on your head, consider the journey that little droplet made from the cloud to the top of your dome. It takes an average-size raindrop about 2 minutes to make its way from the rainclouds—about 2,500 feet (762 m) above ground—all the way down to us! And while smaller raindrops may take more time to hit the ground than larger raindrops, you can count on ALL raindrops to get you wet! So the next time you spy a rain cloud in the sky, you better make sure to run for the ol' umbrella.

What's the Temperature?

Ask a cricket! Did you know that you can guess the temperature outside by counting a cricket's chirps? Here's how: Count the number of a cricket's chirps in 15 seconds. Then, add 40. The result is the approximate outside temperature in degrees Fahrenheit!

Operation: Amateur Meteorologist

Observe the weather conditions where you live, and record a weather report for your friends and family. Is it hot or cold? Dry as the desert or raining cats and dogs? Grab a hairbrush for a microphone, and ask a family member to roll some video. Bonus if you can get an umbrella to flip inside out, because this forecast calls for a 100 percent chance of DRAMA!

⚡ METAMORPHOSIS MYSTERY ⚡

Which of the following statements about CATERPILLARS is the one true WOW?

A) Scientists have special listening devices that help them hear caterpillars burp after eating.

B) Once a caterpillar becomes a butterfly, it forgets all about its life as a caterpillar.

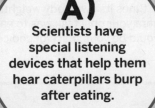

C) Caterpillars have more muscles than humans.

If you guessed C) Caterpillars have more muscles than humans, then CONGRATURITOS! You found the WOW!

Caterpillars actually have A LOT more muscles than humans. Where humans typically have between 640 and 840 muscles, caterpillars can have as many as 4,000 muscles! That should be enough to make you rethink challenging a caterpillar to an arm wrestling match!

The All-You-Can-Eat Caterpillar Cafe

A caterpillar's only job is to . . . EAT! In order for a caterpillar to have enough energy to go through a complete metamorphosis (the process by which it turns into a butterfly), it must eat and eat and eat some more—sometimes as much as 27,000 times its own body weight! Imagine being a caterpillar where your only task was to eat as much as you could. What would be your snack of choice?

Operation: Plant a Butterfly Garden!

Attract new and interesting butterflies to your garden by planting the food that their caterpillars like most. Do a little digging to find out which species of butterfly live in your area. Then visit your local garden center to find the plants that will attract them and their caterpillars. The more caterpillar food you have outside your home, the more butterflies and even birds will come to visit!

⚡ DON'T SWEAT IT! ⚡

Which of the following statements about SWEAT is the one true WOW?

A) Hippo sweat is actually green.

B) Every person's sweat has a unique smell and taste.

C) Horses sweat only through their noses.

If you guessed B) Every person's sweat has a unique smell and taste, then CONGRATURITOS! You found the WOW!

Forget name tags; all you need to tell two different people apart is the olfactory factory between your ears! That's because every single person's sweat has a unique smell and taste. Just like our fingerprints, no one has the same sweat—meaning your sweat can be used to help people identify you based on the way you smell. This is part of how search and rescue dogs typically use their super sense of smell to help find people who are lost in the wilderness.

Sweat Like a Pig?

When it comes to sweat, you're not going to find a whole lot of it on a pig. In fact, pigs hardly sweat at all! While humans use sweat as a way to cool their bodies, to do the same thing, pigs have to bathe in mud. How do you think the phrase "sweat like a pig" came to be?

Operation: Sweat-athon!

Exercise with your family members, and then put on a blindfold and try to identify your family by the smell of their sweat!

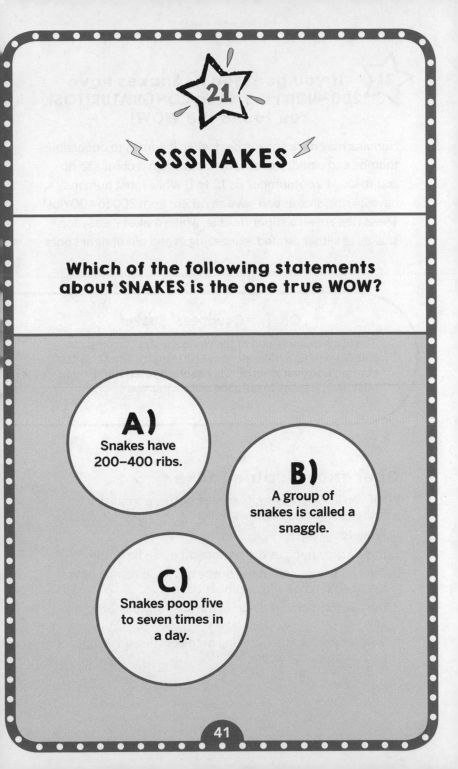

21

⚡ SSSNAKES ⚡

Which of the following statements about SNAKES is the one true WOW?

A)
Snakes have 200–400 ribs.

B)
A group of snakes is called a snaggle.

C)
Snakes poop five to seven times in a day.

41

21 If you guessed A) Snakes have 200–400 ribs, then CONGRATURITOS! You found the WOW!

Humans may have snakes beat when it comes to opposable thumbs and bipedal locomotion, but when it comes to rib count, snakes outnumber us 10 to 1! While most humans have 24 ribs, snakes can have anywhere from 200 to 400 ribs! These ribs are also super flexible, which makes it easy for snakes to slither around, squeezing in and out of tight spots.

Oh, for Goodness' Snake!

The black mamba, one of the world's fastest snakes, can slither up to 12.5 miles per hour (20 kmph)! Time how fast you can ride your bike, or roller-skate, or even run! Do you have what it takes to outpace a black mamba?

Operation: Bubble Snake

What you'll need: an empty plastic bottle, a small cloth, a rubber band, and bubble solution

Wow-to:

1. Have a grownup cut the bottom off a plastic bottle.
2. Cover the wide end of the bottle with a cloth, and hold the cloth in place with a rubber band.
3. Dip the cloth-covered end of the bottle into bubble solution.
4. Gently blow into the opening of the bottle and watch your bubble snake appear!

⚡ TOILET TALK ⚡

Which of the following statements about TOILETS is the one true WOW?

A)
The modern toilet seat was modeled after a Victorian-era fashion accessory.

B)
There is a toilet that makes electricity from pee.

C)
Doctors recommend that people with back pain spend more time sitting on toilets.

22

If you guessed B) There is a toilet that makes electricity from pee, then CONGRATURITOS! You found the WOW!

Researchers from the University of the West of England created a toilet that converts PEE into ELECTRICITY! The technology uses tiny microbes that feed on urine as fuel, break it down, and release electricity. These researchers hope that someday these toilets will make it to parts of the world where people don't have electricity. Now that's some serious pee-pee power!

Toilet . . . MUSEUM?!

Japan has a toilet museum! The TOTO museum features the evolution of toilets from the first ceramic flush seat of 1914 to the most high-tech toilets of today. One highlight includes a toilet that plays sounds to mask "toilet noises." Eww or oooh?!

Operation: The Future of Porcelain Thrones

We challenge you to unclog your mind, take the plunge, and design a toilet of the future! What will it look like? What will it sound like? How will it work? Take some time to "flush out" your most inventive ideas!

⚡ CLOUD JUICE ⚡

Which of the following statements about WATER is the one true WOW?

A) We drink the same water as dinosaurs did.

B) Hot water takes longer to freeze than cold water.

C) It is much harder to swim in syrup than it is in water.

If you guessed A) We drink the same water as dinosaurs did, then CONGRATURITOS! You found the WOW!

We not only drink the same water as dinosaurs, but we also drink the same water as woolly mammoths, our earliest human ancestors, and President George Washington! Earth has been recycling water for roughly 4 billion years and has no more water now than at any other time in history. Water is constantly evaporating and coming back in the form of rain, snow, and sleet. Some water is even trapped in ice sheets. Almost every drop, frozen or not, has been here for billions of years.

Water Wow

Boiling water can turn to ice or snow in midair at -22 degrees Fahrenheit (-30 degrees Celsius).

Operation: Water Bender

Rub an inflated balloon on a rug to build up a static charge, then place that balloon near a faucet of running water. Notice how the water "bends"?

24

⚡ WORM IS THE WORD ⚡

Which of the following statements about WORMS is the one true WOW?

A) A worm once ran for mayor of Talkeetna, Alaska. And WON.

B) Some worms can poop from their mouths.

C) There is a species of worm that exists only in New York City.

24 If you guessed B) Some worms can poop from their mouths, then CONGRATURITOS! You found the WOW!

Worms are truly interesting creatures. They have no arms or legs, they can grow up to 20 feet (6 m) in length, and many species eat their own weight in dirt every single day. But one of the most unusual things about worms is that some of them poop out of their mouths! Meet the hammerhead worm from Malaysia, whose mouth is also its butt. This worm sucks its prey through its mouth, then later POOPS it out of the same opening. Also, if the hammerhead worm is split in two, it can grow into two separate worms. What in the wow?!

Partly Cloudy with a Chance of . . . Raining Worms!?

In southern Norway, it's been known to rain WORMS! But why? While no one knows for sure, one theory is that the worms were swept up into an air pocket and then brought back down miles from where they started. Another theory is that water spouts, similar to tornadoes, traveled through the area, picking up worms and then blowing them out in another area. In addition to worms, it's been known to "rain" fish, snakes, tadpoles, and even birds! What's your theory of raining animals?

Operation: Worm Safari

Next time it rains, step outside and go on a worm hunt near your home. Where might you find some earthworms? Look underneath rocks, logs, backyard furniture, and even toys. When you find one, spend some time observing it. What does it feel like? Can you tell which end is its head? Can you count how many segments it has? Be sure you document your observations in a notebook labeled "Adventure Journal"!

⚡ BIG ANATOMY! ⚡

Which of the following statements about LARGE ANIMALS is the one true WOW?

A)
An elephant's back tooth can grow to 20 inches (51 cm) long.

B)
A fully grown human adult could swim through the veins of a blue whale.

C)
Hippos, on average, can eat up to 3,307 pounds (1.5 tons) of food a day.

25 If you guessed B) A fully grown human adult could swim through the veins of a blue whale, then CONGRATURITOS! You found the WOW!

Blue whales are the largest living animals on the planet! A full-size blue whale can grow up to 100 feet (30 m) long and weigh up to 440,925 pounds (200 tons). That's about the length of two school buses and the weight of 30 elephants. Everything about the blue whale is SUPER SIZED. Its heart is almost the same size and weight as a Harley-Davidson motorcycle, pumping 58 gallons (220 L) of blood at a rate of about 8–10 beats per minute. And the veins and arteries that carry this blood all around the whale's body are large enough for a fully grown adult to swim through!

Whale's Gotta Eat

The blue whale also has an ENORMOUS appetite!

★ Adults eat as much as 8,000 pounds (3.6 tons) of krill a day—that's 40 million krill!

★ Baby blue whales consume up to 150 gallons (568 L) of their mother's milk per day.

If YOU had to eat 8,000 pounds (3.6 tons) of one food for the rest of your life, what would it be?

Operation: Whale of a Tale

Make up your own larger-than-life scientific mystery that involves a blue whale, a library, and a surprise delivery. Be sure to share your whale of a tale with your friends and family!

⚡ THROWING SHADE ⚡

Which of the following statements about SUN SAFETY is the one true WOW?

A)
The parasol was invented over 5,000 years ago in ancient Greece.

B)
Fedoras are the official hat of the U.S Forest Service.

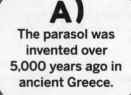

C)
Sunglasses were once used to help judges in ancient China hide their facial expressions.

26 **If you guessed C) Sunglasses were originally used to help judges in ancient China hide their facial expressions, then CONGRATURITOS! You found the WOW!**

An early historical reference to sunglasses dates all the way back to 12th century China. The original design consisted of a slab of smoked quartz, a semi-transparent crystal, roughly attached to the user's face using a wire frame. Although these early sunglasses didn't protect against harmful UV rays, they did come in handy for Chinese judges. These judges wanted to hide their feelings when questioning the accused!

Spectacular Shades

Here's how sunglasses have changed throughout history:

★ In the early 20th century, movie stars started wearing sunglasses on set to protect their eyes from the bright studio lights.

★ In the 1930s, U.S. Air Force pilots wore "aviator" sunglasses to protect their eyes from the harsh glare at high altitudes.

★ It wasn't until the 1950s that sunglasses became more about fashion than protective eyewear.

What would YOU use to try to hide your facial expressions?

Operation: Sun Blocker

Using found objects from around your home, invent a brand new, one-of-a-kind wearable device for blocking the sun's ultraviolet rays! Wear it proudly and don't forget to give it a name.

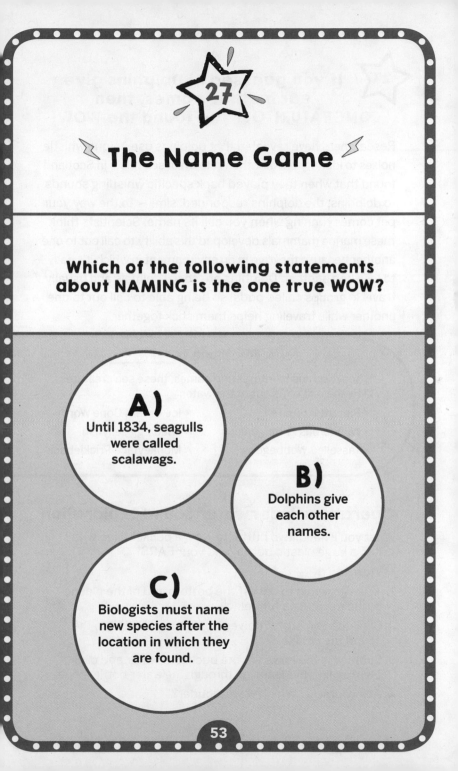

27

⚡ The Name Game ⚡

Which of the following statements about NAMING is the one true WOW?

A)
Until 1834, seagulls were called scalawags.

B)
Dolphins give each other names.

C)
Biologists must name new species after the location in which they are found.

If you guessed B) Dolphins give each other names, then CONGRATURITOS! You found the WOW!

Researchers have revealed that dolphins use unique whistle noises to identify one another. A team of scientists in Scotland found that when they played back specific whistling sounds to dolphins, the dolphins responded, similar to the way your pet comes running when you call its name. Scientists think these marine mammals developed this ability to call out to one another because they live in an environment in which it's easy to lose one another. Dolphins are social animals and usually travel in groups called pods, so being able to call out to one another while traveling helps them stick together.

Hello, My Name Is _____

When it comes to interesting names, these sea creatures blow the rest of us out of the water.

* Pigbutt Worm
* Wunderpus Photogenicus
* Tasselled Wobbegong
* Ice Cream Cone Worm
* Fried Egg Jellyfish
* Monkeyface Prickleback

Operation: Underwater Sound Exploration

What you'll need: two butter knives, a bucket filled with water, a large plastic bottle, and your EARS!

Wow-to:

1. Ask a grownup to cut off the bottom end of the plastic bottle to create a funnel.
2. Clink the two butter knives together and listen to the sound they make.
3. Submerge the knives in the bucket of water and clink them again while listening through the water-bottle funnel.
4. Ask yourself, "Which way is louder?"

28

⚡ NOT YOUR AVERAGE ⚡ SONG AND DANCE

Which of the following statements about MUSIC AND DANCING is the one true WOW?

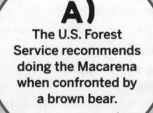

A)
The U.S. Forest Service recommends doing the Macarena when confronted by a brown bear.

B)
Singing opera music has been proven to ease the pain of sore throats.

C)
Playing electronic dance music helps ward off mosquitoes.

If you guessed C) Playing electronic dance music helps ward off mosquitoes, then CONGRATURITOS! You found the WOW!

In an international study, a group of researchers observed the effects of electronic dance music on a type of mosquito called *Aedes aegypti*. The researchers found that the female mosquitoes that were "entertained" by the electronic dance music were less likely to attack hosts, and had less blood-feeding activity. Scientists believe this is because the combination of both high and low frequencies found in electronic dance music interferes with the way mosquitoes signal each other. So the next time you go camping, remember to pack the tent, the deck chairs, and the dubstep!

E-I-E-I-O

Here's how music affects other animals:

★ Some cows produce more milk when listening to slow music.

★ Crocodiles' brains are stimulated by classical music.

★ Dogs that are cooped up inside are happiest when listening to soft rock and reggae, according to one study.

Are there any songs that make YOU behave in a WEIRD way?

Operation: Dancing Grapes

Follow these steps to get your grapes grooving!

What you'll need: a handful of grapes (raisins work well, too), seltzer water, and a vase or mason jar

Wow-to:

1. Fill your vase or mason jar about three-fourths full of seltzer water.

2. Toss in a handful of grapes or raisins.

3. It should take only a few seconds for the grapes or raisins to start "dancing." Cha-cha-cha!

29

CONTINENTAL BREAKFAST

Which of the following statements about CONTINENTS is the one true WOW?

A)
The earth's crust, where the continents sit, is growing thicker over time.

B)
Your fingernails grow at the same rate as the continents move apart.

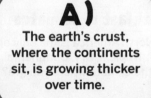

C)
Australia will collide with Africa in 100 million years.

If you guessed B) Your fingernails grow at the same rate as the continents move apart, then CONGRATURITOS! You found the WOW!

You might think of America as being over here, Europe over there, and Australia all the way down under. But about 350 million years ago, all of these landmasses were one big whole, making up a super-continent known as Pangea! However, much like the foam in a bubble bath, these continents are constantly moving and shifting around, but very, VERY slowly—at about the same speed your fingernails are growing. That's about 0.8 inch (20 mm) every year, the diameter of an American 5-cent coin.

A Continental Breakfast of Climates

Of Earth's seven continents, North America is the only one that has every kind of climate: Tropical, Dry, Continental, Moderate, and Polar. What is the climate where you live?

Operation: Pangea Puzzler!

Print a world map and cut out all seven continents as puzzle pieces. Then, piece those continents together to form a recreation of Pangea.

⚡ BARK, BARK, MOO ⚡

Which of the following statements about ANIMAL NOISES is the one true WOW?

A)
Cats reserve their meows for humans, NOT for other cats.

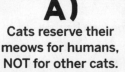

B)
Foxes are often mistaken for wolves by the sound of their deep howls.

C)
Gorillas "sing" to their babies at night.

If you guessed A) Cats reserve their meows for humans, NOT other cats, then CONGRATURITOS! You found the WOW!

Are you kitten me? Turns out that cat meows are just for us humans! Cats use meowing as a way of getting attention when they're upset or hungry. Over the years, cats have honed these meows to be as adorable as possible, to increase their chances of humans helping them. Also, different meows can mean different things. For example, a longer, more throaty meow can indicate worry or annoyance, and endless meowing could indicate illness or injury. If you hear your cat doing that, you should probably take it to the vet . . . right MEOW!

VoCATulary

Clowder: A group of cats
Trichobezoar: The technical name for a hairball
Queen or Molly: A female cat

Operation: Bark! Moo! Hiss!

We all know the noises dogs, cows, and pigs make. But do you know what a mongoose sounds like? How about a zebra, an ostrich, or a porcupine? We challenge you to research the sounds of a variety of different animals. Then, do your best animal impressions to test your family on their random animal-noise knowledge!

PUKE-A-DOODLE-DOO

Which of the following statements about VOMIT is the one true WOW?

A) A pint of great white shark vomit once sold for $70,000.

B) Flies vomit when they land on food.

C) Male cheetahs roll around in their own vomit to attract mates.

31 — If you guessed B) Flies vomit when they land on food, then CONGRATURITOS! You found the WOW!

Most people like to set a nice table before eating. Flies, on the other hand, prefer to barf on their food. When a fly lands on its food, it immediately pukes up a mixture of saliva and stomach acids. This sour solution helps to break down the food, turning solids into a liquid that the fly can then slurp up and eat smoothie-style!

Barf Machine

Researchers at the University of North Carolina built a barfing machine to help them study norovirus, an illness that causes vomiting and diarrhea. Anything for science!

Operation: Toss Your Cookies!

While the phrase "toss your cookies" is commonly used as another way of saying "vomit," we challenge you to use this phrase *literally*! Using different materials found around your home (such as aluminum foil, cardboard, and clay), make a batch of inedible "cookies." Once you've finished your batch, gather family and friends to take turns tossing them. Make predictions as to which cookie will fly the fastest and the farthest. Winner keeps all the cookies! Just remember: DON'T EAT THEM.

32

⚡ SLOW-DOWN SLOTHS ⚡

Which of the following statements about SLOTHS is the one true WOW?

A)
Sloths are closely related to one of the fastest animal species on Earth, the brown hare.

B)
Sloths can hold their pee for 156 hours.

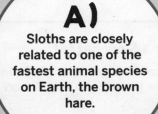

C)
Sloths are some of the sweatiest animals on the planet.

32 If you guessed B) Sloths can hold their pee for 156 hours, then CONGRATURITOS! You found the WOW!

Next time you're busting for the bathroom, imagine having to hold it in, sloth-style! Two-toed sloths can hold their pee for up to 156 hours! This is because sloths live in trees, and every time they go to the bathroom, they put themselves at risk of predators by climbing down from the safety of their high branches. In order to keep their time on the ground to a minimum, sloths hold on to their pee and poop for as long as they can, going to the bathroom only when absolutely necessary. If you're wondering why sloths don't just poop from their perch in the trees, you're not alone! Biologists still haven't been able to crack the mystery of why the sloth makes this dangerous journey down to the jungle floor to do its business.

Talk About a Slow Eater!

It can take a sloth up to 30 days to digest ONE LEAF! On average, how long does it take you to finish your dinner?

Operation: Chew with Your Mouth Slow

Sloths do everything slowly, especially eating! Some experts suggest that we humans should slow down when eating, too, by chewing each bite of food about 32 times before swallowing. During your next meal, count your chews per bite, and see if you can make it to 32, or even more. Challenge a family member to see who can finish their food in the *most* amount of time!

64

⚡ PLAY WITH YOUR FOOD! ⚡
(FOR SCIENCE)

Which of the following statements about FOOD is the one true WOW?

A) Scientists have successfully turned peanut butter into diamonds.

B) Isaac Newton was hit on the head by a pear when he discovered gravity.

C) Chewing gum was originally invented as a filler for cavities.

If you guessed A) Scientists have successfully turned peanut butter into diamonds, then CONGRATURITOS! You found the WOW!

Diamonds are formed deep underground when densely packed carbon atoms come under A LOT of pressure. But everything you need to make a diamond can be found in your kitchen cupboard! Back in 2014, a German scientist named Dan Frost was trying to recreate the same conditions found deep inside the earth in his lab. He needed a carbon-rich material to do this, and, as it turned out, peanut butter was perfect for the job. Frost subjected the peanut butter to high pressures like those found underground. After the experiment was finished, Frost observed that diamonds had formed.

That's Nuts!

Peanut butter isn't only good for munching and making diamonds. Check out these other bizarre uses for peanut butter:

★ Clogging the bottom of an ice cream cone

★ Shaving cream

★ Leather cleaner

★ Gum removal

★ Cockroach bait

What problem could YOU solve with a single scoop of peanut butter?

Operation: Black Light Banana!

Due to the breakdown in chlorophyll, the green pigment found in all green plants, ripe green bananas glow BLUE under ultraviolet black lights! Chlorophyll is responsible for absorbing light to provide the plant with energy for photosynthesis, the process by which plants make food. And while scientists don't know for sure what causes this blue glow, there's a theory that it's to help signal to certain UV-seeing animals that these bananas are ripe for the pickin'!

⚡ JUST IN TIME ⚡

Which of the following statements about TIMEKEEPING is the one true WOW?

A) A clock in Germany has been keeping time for over a thousand years.

B) A jiffy is a scientific unit of time.

C) At the South Pole, clocks tick counterclockwise.

If you guessed B) A jiffy is a scientific unit of time, then CONGRATURITOS! You found the WOW!

As it turns out, a jiffy is a real unit of time used by physicists all over the world. The word "jiffy" apparently dates back to the late 18th century when it was sometimes used as a slang term for lightning. It wasn't until about a century and a half later that chemist Gilbert Newton Lewis used the term "jiffy" to define the amount of time it takes for light to travel 0.4 inch (1 cm) in a vacuum. Which is quick. Really, REALLY quick! Just one 50th of a second!

More Than Just a Jiffy

Here are some of Gilbert Newton Lewis's other scientific accomplishments:

★ He created the term "photon," which refers to the particles that light is made of.

★ He discovered covalent bonds, which hold two atoms together.

★ He was nominated for the Nobel Prize 41 times, although he never won.

If you could rename the jiffy, what would YOU call it?

Operation: PENder Bender

Watch light bend in a jiffy with this experiment!

Wow-to:

1. Fill a glass or jar half full with water.
2. Drop a pencil into the jar.
3. Observe the pencil through the side of the jar. Does it appear to be bent? This is an optical illusion. Because light can't travel as quickly through water, as the light is bending around the pencil it's causing the pencil to appear bent.

A BONE TO PICK WITH YOU

Which of the following statements about BONES is the one true WOW?

A)
Half the bones in the human body are found in the foot.

B)
The South American bullfrog has more bones than any other animal.

C)
A cubic inch (16 cm^3) of human bone can withstand the weight of five standard pickup trucks.

If you guessed C) A cubic inch (16 cm³) of human bone can withstand the weight of five standard pickup trucks, then CONGRATURITOS! You found the WOW!

Bones are some of the strongest materials found in nature. Ounce for ounce, they're about four times stronger than concrete and five times stronger than steel. Just 1 cubic inch (16 cm³) of our bones' structure can bear loads of up to 19,000 pounds (8,618 kg)! That's about as heavy as five standard pickup trucks!

Beefed-Up Bones

The human body has 206 bones, but some are stronger than others. The top three strongest bones inside YOU are:

1. Femur
2. Temporal bone
3. Tibia

Have YOU ever broken a bone? What helped it to heal?

Operation: Build-A-Bone

The backbone, or the spine, is an essential part of the human body that makes it possible for us to stand up, bend over, and walk. We challenge you to build a model of the human backbone.

What you'll need: an egg carton, a pair of scissors, and pipe cleaners or yarn

Wow-to:

1. Use the scissors to cut the egg carton into 12 sections or cups.

2. Poke a hole in each cup, and thread the cups together using the pipe cleaners or yarn. Continue threading until all 12 cups are fastened together.

3. Compare your model with an image of an actual human backbone!

36

⚡ **DON'T GO BREAKING MY HEART** ⚡

Which of the following statements about beating HEARTS is the one true WOW?

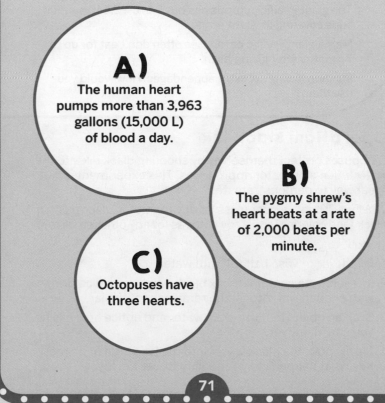

A)
The human heart pumps more than 3,963 gallons (15,000 L) of blood a day.

B)
The pygmy shrew's heart beats at a rate of 2,000 beats per minute.

C)
Octopuses have three hearts.

36 If you guessed C) Octopuses have three hearts, then CONGRATURITOS! You found the WOW!

The octopus is an interesting-looking creature from the outside, but take a look inside and things get BONKERBALLS! For example, the giant Pacific octopus has THREE HEARTS. WHAT in the WOW?! The octopus has two hearts that pump blood directly to each of its gills and then a larger heart to circulate its blue blood throughout the rest of its body.

Some More to Octopi Your Mind

Other unusual facts about everyone's favorite eight-armed cephalopods:

★ The octopus uses puffs of ink to escape its predators.

★ The giant Pacific octopus has has 2,140—2,240 suction cups covering its eight arms.

★ Mama giant Pacific octopuses often don't eat for up to 7 months after giving birth.

Imagine having six extra appendages. How would you use them?

Operation: Black Ink

Octopuses protect themselves by shooting black ink into the water when a predator approaches. This experiment is a great way to demonstrate it.

What you'll need: a clear glass jar or vase, water, black paint or black food coloring, and a toy octopus (or any other small toy)

Wow-to:

1. Fill the jar or vase half full with water.

2. In a separate container, mix black paint or food coloring with enough water to fill the remainder of the jar.

3. Drop an object into the plain water and notice how easily you can identify it.

4. Slowly pour the black water into the jar a little at a time. See what happens to your ability to see the toy.

37

⚡ CLASSIC CONDIMENTS ⚡

Which of the following statements about CONDIMENTS is the one true WOW?

A)
Mustard was named after a famous colonel who died in World War I.

B)
Relish was outlawed in Illinois from 1945 to 1962.

C)
Ketchup was once used as a medicine to treat diarrhea.

If you guessed C) Ketchup was once used as a medicine to treat diarrhea, then CONGRATURITOS! You found the WOW!

The word "ketchup" comes from the Hokkien Chinese word "kê-tsiap," a fermented fish sauce. However, it wasn't until 1834 that Dr. John Cooke Bennet decided to market the condiment as a medicine. His original tomato sauce was said to cure diarrhea and indigestion, and it didn't come in a bottle—it came in pill form! Although Bennet's health claims were a bit exaggerated, tomato ketchup is a great source of lycopene, an antioxidant naturally found in tomatoes that can help improve heart health.

Once upon a Time

Ketchup isn't the only household item that was originally intended for other purposes.

★ Coca-Cola was originally sold as a tonic that could relieve stress and make you smarter.

★ Listerine was once sold as a disinfectant to clean floors.

★ Frisbees were originally pie containers.

   What would YOU use ketchup for?

Operation: Blindfolded Condiment Taste Test

Grab a grownup, put on a blindfold, and have your grownup help you taste different condiments that represent salty (such as barbecue sauce), sweet (such as strawberry jam), bitter (such as unsweetened cocoa), and sour (such as dill pickle relish). Guess what each flavor is. Try it again; this time holding your nose while you taste. Notice a difference? When it comes to taste, your tongue teams up with your nose!